The Buildings of Shrewsbury

1 The English Bridge was designed by John Gwynne and built between 1768 and 1774. In the 1920s the bridge was completely dismantled, but at the suggestion of A.W. Ward the basic design was repeated in the new bridge. Most of the original facing stones were carefully re-used. On the far bank is the Congregational church built in 1863 to the designs of G. Bidlake of Wolverhampton.

The Buildings of Shrewsbury

R ICHARD K. M ORRISS

With photographs by Ken Hoverd

ALAN SUTTON

First published in the United Kingdom in 1993 by
Alan Sutton Publishing Limited
Phoenix Mill · Far Thrupp · Stroud · Gloucestershire

First published in the United States of America in 1993 by
Alan Sutton Publishing Inc · 83 Washington Street · Dover · NH 03820

British Library Cataloguing in Publicaton Data

Morriss, Richard K.
  Buildings of Shrewsbury
  I. Title
  720.942454

  ISBN 0-7509-0253-1

Library of Congress Cataloging in Publication Data applied for

*Cover photographs: front, a fine late medieval building on the
corner of Mardol and Roushill, probably late fifteenth century
(inset, Market Hall); back, Barracks Passage off Wyle Cop.*

Typeset in 11/14 Times.
Typesetting and origination by
Alan Sutton Publishing Limited.
Printed in Great Britain by
Redwood Books, Trowbridge, Wiltshire

Contents

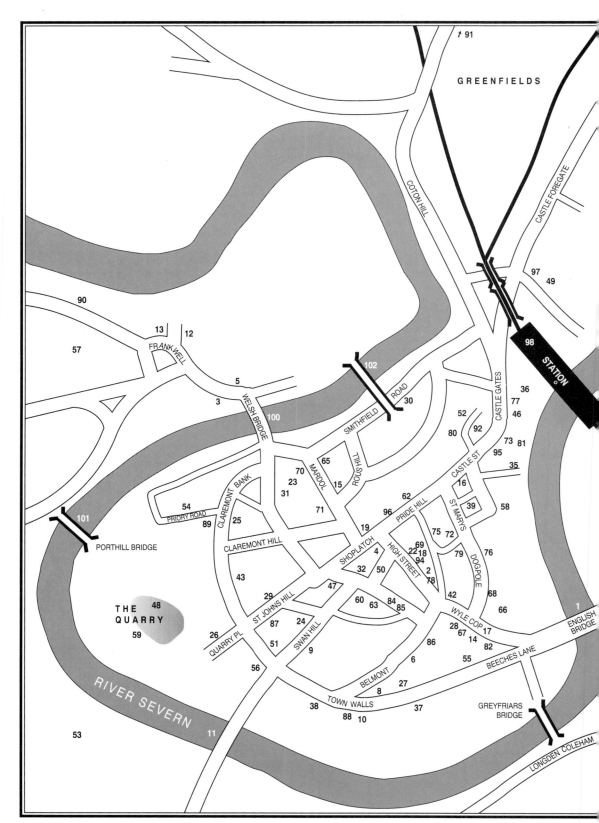

91

GREENFIELDS

CASTLE FOREGATE

COTON HILL

90

13 12

57

FRANKWELL

5

3

WELSH BRIDGE

100

102

SMITHFIELD

ROAD

30

97 49

98 STATION

CASTLE GATES

36

77

46

52

80 92

CASTLE ST

73 81

95

35

101

PORTHILL BRIDGE

54

PRIORY ROAD

89

CLAREMONT BANK

25

CLAREMONT HILL

65

70

23

31

MARDOL

15

ROUSHILL

71

62

96 PRIDE HILL

19

16

39

58

ST MARYS

75 72

DOGPOLE

79 76

68

66

1

ENGLISH BRIDGE

THE QUARRY

48

59

43

29

ST JOHNS HILL

47

26

QUARRY PL

87 24

51

SWAN HILL

9

56

SHOPLATCH

4

32 50

HIGH STREET

60 63

84 85

42

69

22 18

94

2

78

28 67 17

14 82

BEECHES LANE

86

55

6

27

BELMONT

8

38 TOWN WALLS

88 10

37

GREYFRIARS BRIDGE

WYLE COP

RIVER SEVERN

11

53

LONGDEN COLEHAM

(Numbers relate to caption numbers in text)

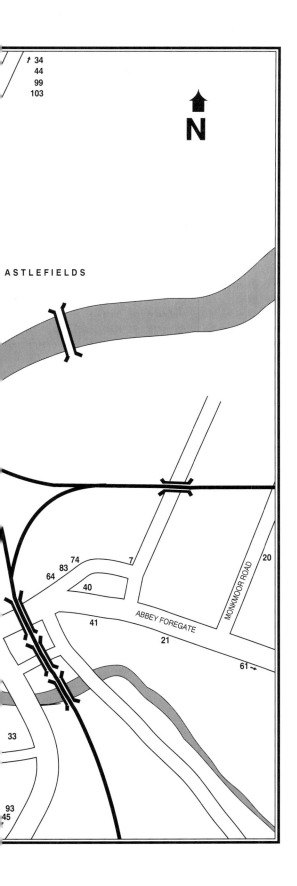

ASTLEFIELDS

34
44
99
103

N

74
83
64
7
40
41
21
33
93
45

MONKMOOR ROAD
ABBEY FOREGATE
20
61

Introduction

The towne of Shrobbesbyri standithe on a rokky hill of
stone of a sadde redd earth, and Severne so girdethe in all
the towne that savinge a litle pece by . . . it wer an isle.

(John Leland, c. 1535)

Shrewsbury occupies an ideal defensive site that no early settlers
appear to have made use of. In the Iron Age the regional centre
of the local tribe, the Cornovii, was a hill-fort on the Wrekin.
Towards the end of the first century AD the conquering Romans
built their new regional capital, Uriconium, on the banks of the
Severn a few miles downstream. From the traces in the village of
Wroxeter it is difficult to believe that, for over three hundred
years, this was one of the largest cities in Britain. A road leading
westwards from Uriconium passed just to the south of
Shrewsbury, and recent excavations near Meole Brace uncovered
traces of a small roadside settlement.

As the Roman Empire disintegrated, the legions left Britain
and the province was left to fend for itself. Uriconium was aban-
doned by the fifth century and the new British kingdom of
Powys emerged. Traditionally its capital, Pengwern, is thought
to have been Shrewsbury, the palace standing on the site of old
St Chad's. In the seventh century it was burnt to the ground by
the invading English but, so far, there has been no archaeological
evidence to indicate that this really was Shrewsbury.

It is true that the Britons who lived in this area were gradually
forced further and further westwards into Wales by the Anglo-
Saxon settlers. When Offa's Dyke was built as a boundary mark-
er in the eighth century, Shrewsbury was well within the English
kingdom of Mercia. By this time there was a growing settlement
within the river loop and in 901 it was classed as a *civitas*,
or administrative centre. The origins of its Saxon name,

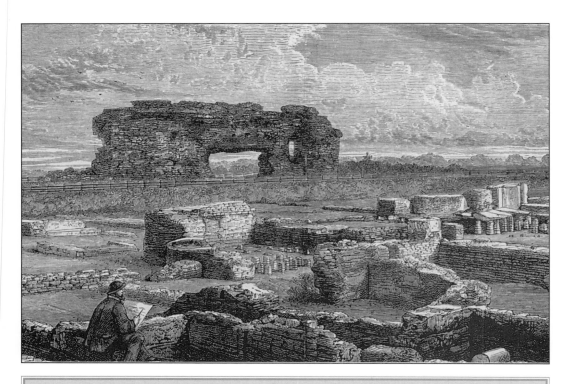

Uriconium was one of the largest cities in Roman Britain and the predecessor of Shrewsbury as the regional centre. It has been attracting the interest of antiquaries for generations, this engraving dating from the late 1870s.

Scrobbesbyrig, are unclear. 'Scrobb' may have been a person, or could mean scrub or brush; the byrig or burh ending implies that the town was fortified.

Shrewsbury flourished in the peace of the late Saxon period. Naturally well defended, it commanded an important river crossing and developed as an important regional trading centre. When, in the late tenth century, local government was reorganized into shires, Shrewsbury became the county town of Shropshire. By the reign of Edward the Confessor it had at least 252 houses, five churches, three mills, and a mint. Its population was probably about two thousand – a sizeable town in the eleventh century.

Evidence of this busy phase of the town's history is frustratingly scarce. Within the river loop the higher land is almost split into two by the valley of a small stream that once ran westwards

The defences of Shrewsbury are well illustrated by this eighteenth-century view of the castle and Castle Foregate, seen from Coton Hill. To the right of the castle is the Castle Gate and a section of town wall.

to the river, roughly along the line of the present High Street. The earliest Saxon settlement was probably on the southern portion of high land, around the oldest church, St Chad's. The later burh occupied the land to the north of the stream, nearer to the neck of the loop, and may have been founded by Queen Aethelflaeda of Mercia in the early tenth century. There was also some Saxon settlement in what is now the Abbey Foregate area, particularly near to the old ford.

After the Normans conquered England in 1066 they quickly appreciated the strategic importance of Shrewsbury. Shropshire was given to Roger de Montgomery, a close friend of William the Conqueror, as a semi-independent county palatine that Roger, the first Earl of Shrewsbury, ruled like a prince. By the end of the century the town had the two important elements in any significant medieval town – a strong castle, guarding the

Shrewsbury Abbey was
founded in the late
eleventh century by
Roger de Montgomery,
who entered it as a lay
brother shortly before
his death. Despite being
rebuilt, partly
demolished, and
heavily restored in its
turbulent past, much of
the Norman work
survives, as shown in
this engraving of 1826.

neck of the loop, and a new abbey, just across the river ford to the east.

The Normans destroyed part of the Saxon town to build the castle, but probably kept much of the basic street pattern. They also established two major suburbs outside the river loop, next to each of the two river crossings. To the west was Frankwell, on the road to Wales. Despite its name this was unlikely to have been a suburb occupied by the French-speakers mentioned in the Domesday survey, especially as there are no surviving French names in the area. Known as 'the Little Borough', Frankwell was outside the jurisdiction of the town.

To the east was the Abbey Foregate, owned and administered by the abbey. The abbey and town were often in dispute and jealously guarded their privileges, particularly over corn milling. Unlike most of Shrewsbury, the Abbey Foregate suburb was laid

out on a definite plan, with narrow burgage plots running at right angles to the main road leading eastwards from the abbey. This type of urban plantation was designed to bring in rents to help fill the abbey's coffers. Abbey Foregate was thus a separate borough, with its own rules and its own market-place, north of the abbey church, later known as the Horsefair.

As a key strategic town in the pacification and control of Wales, and as the main marketing centre for Welsh wool, Shrewsbury continued to thrive in the centuries that followed the Conquest. It was still vulnerable to attack and was twice burnt by the Welsh in the early thirteenth century. Nevertheless, bridges had replaced both fords by the twelfth century and the town was walled by the middle of the thirteenth. After the ending of the intermittent Welsh wars in 1284 the town became a much safer place to live in and to trade from. By the start of the following century Shrewsbury was

Shrewsbury's abbey was often at odds with the town itself. The abbey developed its own planned settlement along Abbey Foregate. This view from around 1900 shows a forgotten – pre-motor car – age when the main danger to pedestrians was also good for rhubarb. Dawdling across Abbey Foregate today is not recommended.

John Gwynne's English Bridge, seen here in an early twentieth-century postcard, before it was taken down and rebuilt. His Atcham Bridge, a few miles downstream, still survives and is very similar in style.

one of the wealthiest towns in England, and its rich wool merchants travelled far and wide.

Until the mid-thirteenth century the main market had taken place in the streets around St Alkmund's. In the early 1270s a new, paved market area was laid out between the two areas of high ground. Now known as the Square, this became the new focus of the still-growing town. More streets were laid out to fill in the hitherto empty areas within the town, including, by the thirteenth century, Mardol, which also appears to have had planned burgage plots along it. Between the medieval streets were narrow passages, locally still known as shuts – probably an abbreviated form of 'short cut'. Many of these remain, providing useful short cuts for those that know their way around the town. There was also further suburban development outside the river loop, in Coton to the north and Coleham to the south.

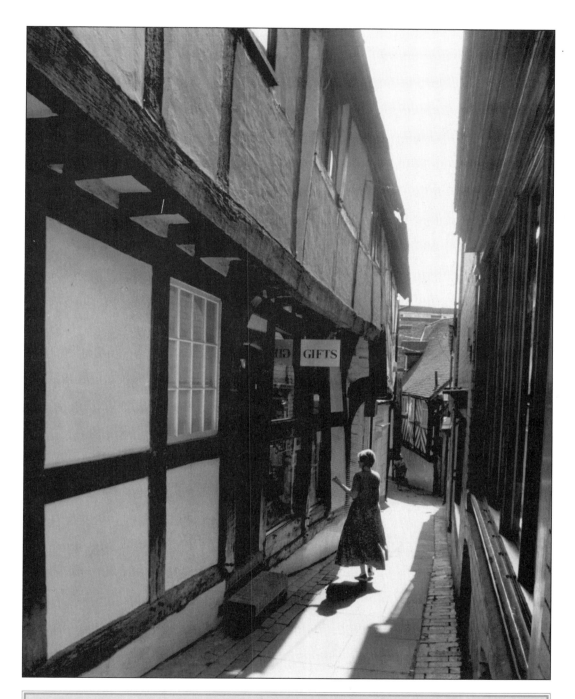

2 Grope Lane evokes medieval Shrewsbury and probably got its name from people 'groping' down the dark alleyway or 'shut'. Ancient jettied timber-framed buildings still line it, but the paving would have been an unheard of luxury in such a street.

3 The Fellmongers, in the suburb of Frankwell, is a reminder of Shrewsbury's wool trade. It was built in the 1580s, with separate accommodation units on the upper floors above four separate ground-floor shops. Behind the close-studded and jettied frontage block was the much plainer wool-store and workshops. Fellmongering, the processing of sheepskins, continued on this site until 1971. Since 1979 it has been owned by the Civic Society and has been renovated.

The Black Death came to Britain in 1348 and, in several epidemics, devastated the country. Well over a third of the population perished, and Shrewsbury seems to have suffered badly. Its fortunes were not helped by a downturn in the market for Welsh wool. In the fourteenth century the Welsh wool producers began to sell their raw wool to a growing Welsh woollen industry, rather than exporting it all to Shrewsbury. The Welsh also found buyers for their cloth in other border towns, such as Welshpool and Oswestry. By the early fifteenth century Shrewsbury was one of several towns in which 'diverse and many houses messuages and tenements . . . now for a long time have been in great ruin and decay . . .'.

Even the once wealthy abbey and the friaries suffered from the town's declining fortunes. When Henry VIII dissolved them in the 1530s they were struggling to survive. The abbey had just seventeen monks, its roof leaked, and the abbot was demolishing buildings and selling materials to pay off debts. Only three brothers were left at the Austin Friars, and the Greyfriars had 'no jewels, but a plate cross silver, and one little chalice of little value'. Only the Blackfriars bothered to put up much of a protest when the final orders came for them to close.

By the middle of the sixteenth century the town's population was around two and a half thousand – about half of what it had been two centuries earlier. There then followed a quite remarkable recovery in the last few decades of the century, so much so that by the start of the seventeenth century the population had doubled to reach the five thousand mark. No doubt much of this revival was due to the general economic upturn of the Elizabethan age when the religious uncertainties following the Reformation were left, temporarily, behind and the nation prospered.

Shrewsbury's new wealth was still based on wool, but this time on the virtual monopoly on the marketing of cheap Welsh woollen cloth held by the Drapers Company. The woven cloth came in from the cottages and farmsteads of North and Mid Wales on pack-horses to be sold in the Market Square. It would then be cut and pressed in Shrewsbury and sent on to London for resale and, often, for export. The fairly modest headquarters of the powerful Drapers Company, built in the 1570s, still stands in St Mary's Square and most of the fine timber-framed houses in

4 Ireland's Mansion, in High Street, was built by Robert Ireland, a wool merchant, in the late sixteenth century and has the most sophisticated of the timber-framed façades in the town. Apart from decorative bargeboards and some cable-moulding, the building's main effect comes from its lavish use of timber, its sheer size, and its symmetry. It has been re-windowed with Georgian sashes.

5 This house in Frankwell, near to the Welsh Bridge, is a fine example of late sixteenth-century timber framing. At an unknown date the frame was hidden behind lath and plaster and only exposed again earlier this century.

6 At the end of the seventeenth century Shrewsbury had become a rather elegant place to live – if you were wealthy enough – and Belmont was one of the best streets in which to reside. No. 10 Belmont was built in this period and has survived remarkably unchanged. The rather tall windows, thick glazing bars, crown glass, overhanging roof and plain string course are all typical of the date. The three ground-floor windows to the right of the door are all 'blind' – simply painted to look like the real thing. Like so many houses in the town, the house has been converted into offices.

7 Abbeydale House in Abbey Foregate, to the north-east of the abbey, is very similar in design and date to No. 10 Belmont. Unfortunately, much of its charm has been ruined by the removal of its original multi-paned sashes and their replacement with large and soul-less plate glass. The house was for many years owned by the local Health Authority but was awaiting a new use in 1992.

the town belonged to drapers or others connected with the wool trade. Other important buildings of this date include the new Market Hall and the former Grammar School.

Religious and political turmoil resurfaced in England in the middle years of the seventeenth century and resulted in the Civil War. Charles I raised his standard at Nottingham in the summer of 1642. Soon afterwards he marched to Shrewsbury to muster support – and money – and stayed for several weeks. A mint was established in the town and for a time Prince Rupert himself was in charge of the garrison. Throughout the war, Shropshire's Royalist strongholds fell one by one, Shrewsbury itself being taken in February 1645.

The town shared the same uncertainty that the whole country endured throughout the Commonwealth, but began to recover soon after the Restoration of 1660. The wool trade itself became gradually less and less important as the town began to meet the needs of a more prosperous population. Luxury trades such as bookbinding, watchmaking and tailoring grew, and in 1695 the town had twelve barbers, a miniature-portrait painter and two dancing masters. It had become a much more genteel place, so much so that when the redoubtable traveller Celia Fiennes visited, in 1698, she could report that 'the ladies and gentlemen, walk [in the abbey gardens] as in St James' Park, and there are abundance of people of quality living in Shrewsbury, more than in any town except Nottingham'. Twenty years or so later, Defoe called it 'a Town of Mirth and Gallantry . . . one of the most flourishing Towns in England'.

Shrewsbury prospered throughout the eighteenth century and its wealth is reflected in its elegant Georgian buildings. As county town it held the quarter sessions four times a year and the assizes twice a year; many county landowners kept up town houses in Shrewsbury for these events and for the 'season'. The social needs of the gentry were met by coffee houses and by assembly rooms in the better hotels, the best surviving being that in the Lion Hotel. The most precious legacy of the Georgian season is undoubtedly the town's famous Quarry Park, laid out with tree-lined walks by the river in 1719 for promenading, and still undefiled by building or development. The town began to expand again and new high-status development took place around old St Chad's, Belmont, Swan Hill, St John's Hill, and, towards the end

8 The gazebo or belvedere was a feature of Georgian country houses and was used as an intimate little home from home for picnics and entertainments. Some were built in towns, including this one of Town Walls that belonged to a house fronting Belmont. It was probably built in the 1720s, or possibly slightly earlier. It was restored recently and converted into a small house.

9 Swan Hill Court, a typical quiet back street in the fashionable Georgian quarter that developed in the early eighteenth century. It is now a fine example of modern urban conservation.

of the century, along the course of the old town wall overlooking the Quarry Park.

In the 1790s Shrewsbury looked like becoming an industrial town. The Severn, navigable from Wales to the Bristol Channel, was then one of the busiest rivers in Europe and there were ambitious plans to link it by canal to the Dee and Mersey. Another canal linked the town to the industrial region in the east of the country. Two large flax mills were built to the north of the town and a woollen mill was opened in Coleham near to William Hazeldine's new foundry. Fortunately, for posterity at least, these industrial concerns did not expand to any great extent and Shrewsbury remained a rural county town.

In the early nineteenth century this lack of industrial expansion was partly the cause of another decline in the town's fortunes, particularly in the 1830s. In that decade the population fell from over twenty-one thousand to just over eighteen thousand, when most towns were experiencing population growth. This proved to be a short-lived downturn, and from the 1850s the town continued to expand and prosper again, helped to a large extent by the arrival of the railways from 1848 onwards.

Major public improvements were made. Gas lighting first appeared in the 1820s, proper sewers were started in the 1850s, a power station opened in 1895, and there was a continuous programme of road improvements throughout the century. Two other significant redevelopments improved the town's markets. A large new stock market, or Smithfield, was opened on the former Raven Meadows in 1850, and a new general market opened off Shoplatch in 1869.

Towards the end of the century Shrewsbury dramatically increased in size. The overcrowded and unsanitary poorer parts of the centre of the town were gradually cleared away. Planned developments of artisans' houses grew up just outside the town centre, including Castlefields and Greenfields to the north, and Cherry Orchard to the east. The opening of the Kingsland Bridge in 1883, coupled with the move of Shrewsbury School to Kingsland, led to the development of leafy middle-class housing on what had once been rough pasture overlooking the town.

Inevitably, the twentieth century has seen Shrewsbury lose some of its individuality as mass-production and mass—

10 A late-Victorian cast-iron drinking fountain in Town Walls, with a typical message of the time beneath the single Salopian 'Loggerhead'.

transportation erode regional differences. Its new suburbs could have been built on the outskirts of any town, and have swallowed up outlying villages such as Meole Brace, Shelton and Sutton. Huge inroads have been made into the surrounding countryside in a process that continues unabated as the century draws to a close. Within the town centre, the need to satisfy the requirements of the motor car has resulted in traffic improvements and car parks to the detriment of architecture and ambience.

Despite all this the town centre has kept much of its unique character, its medieval street pattern, many of its historic buildings, and its ancient open spaces. Strolling in the Quarry Park, looking across the river to the cattle grazing on the Kingsland bank, it is easy to forget that you are in the middle of a large town. The ease with which the urban changes to the rural is part of Shrewsbury's charm.

11 Kingsland Bridge was built by a private company in 1883 after several schemes had previously failed. It is a 'bow-string' bridge with the segmental iron arch, 65 metres long, supporting a suspended roadway. The bridge was a key element in the development of middle-class suburbs in Kingsland. It is still privately owned and modern automatic toll-barriers have recently replaced the toll-keepers.

An array of typical Georgian doorcases. Top left: School Gardens, right: Belmont. Bottom left: Quarry Place, right: St John's Hill.

Architectural Character

The architectural character of any town is governed by several different factors – the layout of its streets, the survival rate of its historic buildings, and the building materials used in them. Shrewsbury has managed to retain much of its medieval street pattern, as well as far more of its historic buildings than most towns of its size. However, all of those buildings have had to adapt over the centuries to the changing status and needs of their owners. The result is a fascinating townscape representing a thousand years of architectural development.

The oldest surviving buildings in Shrewsbury – the abbey, churches, castle, town walls and remnants of larger medieval houses – are all built of stone. This gives a very misleading impression, for most buildings up to the late seventeenth century would have been timber framed, and the majority simply have not survived. The local stone is a deep-red carboniferous sandstone, known as Keele Bed Sandstone, seen in the castle, the town walls, the abbey and St Mary's church. The abbey and St Mary's also contain a different variety of New Red Sandstone, quarried from outcrops a few miles to the north.

Shropshire was once a well-wooded county, and timber, especially oak, was a natural material for building construction. Timber-framed buildings were normally pre-fabricated, the timbers being measured, sawn and temporarily slotted together on the floor of the carpenter's yard. Individual joints were then numbered, usually in Roman numerals, so that when the timbers were carted to the building site, the frames could be put back together in the right way. These carpenters' marks can often be seen scratched or gouged into the faces of the timbers.

12 A medieval cruck frame is exposed in the gable end of 92 Frankwell, an otherwise undistinguished brick-faced cottage. This very simple type of construction depended on all the framing for the side walls being supported by the paired crucks.

13 Medieval box-framing usually had very large panels that needed to be braced for stability. Tucked away behind a house in Frankwell is a short two-bay range of unknown date, possibly fourteenth century.

Most of the surviving timber-framed buildings in Shrewsbury are of box-frame construction, and often jettied. The jettying out of one or more of the upper floors on one or more sides is common. It was not, as is often thought, done to increase floor space, but helped to make the upper floors more stable because of the weight distribution of the jettied frames. Jetties tended to get shallower towards the end of the sixteenth century.

The more primitive-looking cruck frame survives in buildings in Frankwell and Abbey Foregate. There is still considerable debate about the dating of cruck frames, and all that can be said with any degree of certainty is that Shrewsbury's rare examples are medieval. In a cruck frame, a large timber – often the main bough of a tree – is sawn in half to produce two identically shaped pieces of timber. These are then joined by a collar beam to form an A-frame from which everything else in the building is supported.

14 This fourteenth-century crown-post roof was rediscovered during recent restoration work in the Trotting Horse fronting Barrack's Passage, off Wyle Cop. This type of roof relied on trussed rafters resting on a central purlin, supported by the central crown-posts on the tie beams. Later roofs had side purlins supported on main trusses, as in most modern buildings.

The panels in medieval timber-framing were very large, and braces, usually curved and sometimes cusped, often had to be introduced into the framing to keep it rigid. Gradually the size of the panels was reduced, until the decorative panels on a building such as Owen's Mansion in the High Street were very small indeed. The panels were infilled with wattle and daub. Staves were fitted into a series of drilled holes in the underside of the upper rail of the panel and then sprung into a long groove on the top of the lower rail. Pliable branches were then woven between the staves to complete the key (the wattle) for the daub – an often horrendous mixture of dung, clay and animal hair. This was covered by a thin plaster skin.

Another type of framing that became popular, particularly in the sixteenth century, was close-studding. Vertical posts, or studs, in the frame were placed very close together, usually only

15 On the corner of Mardol and Roushill, this late medieval building probably dates to the early fifteenth century. It has typically large medieval panels with curved braces. It was jettied on the Roushill frontage, to the right. The Mardol frontage seems to have been remodelled in the sixteenth century to appear more up to date. If a building is jettied on two or more sides a special timber, known as the dragon beam, is needed at the corners. When the building was restored recently, it was given a rather different type of dragon beam – a witty conceit.

16 The close-studding of Perche's Mansion was hidden behind plaster until quite recently. The house was built in 1581 for John Perche, four-times bailiff of the town. The front onto Castle Street is hidden by later buildings, but even this plain side elevation was impressive, with shallow jettied first and second floors. The ground floor was later extended into the street and the first-floor jetty underbuilt in brick.

the same distance as their width away from the next stud. It was a deliberately expensive use of timber and was usually only seen on the main fronts of buildings. Typical examples of close-studding are Mytton's Mansion in Wyle Cop, and Ireland's Mansion in the High Street.

Towards the end of the sixteenth century the nation's timber reserves were dwindling rapidly because of increased use of charcoal for iron-smelting and an upsurge in the demand from the construction industry. To conserve stocks and ensure sufficient timbers for the Navy, various measures were passed to limit its use in construction. Paradoxically, in Shrewsbury the buildings of the richer drapers and merchants of this period show an increasingly lavish use of timber as they tried to outdo each other in the ostentatious display of their new-found wealth. A local school of carpentry flourished, using motifs such as

17 Wyle Cop, one of the finest urban views in England, climbs up from the English Bridge into the centre of town. The scene constantly changes as you climb the hill. On the left is the 36.5 metre frontage of Mytton's Mansion, the left-hand side of which is still encased with lath and plaster, as is the Nag's Head opposite. Beyond the Henry Tudor House near the top of the hill is the Lion Hotel. Only the constant flow of traffic spoils the effect.

18 In complete contrast to the wide sweep of Wyle Cop are the town's medieval narrow shuts or alleyways. Golden Cross Passage runs between the High Street and the churchyard of old St Chad's.

19 A less than typical example of brick cladding of a timber frame on Mardol Head. The small two-storey, timber-framed building in Mardol is probably sixteenth century in date. The huge, decorative, Flemish-style half gable belongs to an early eighteenth-century five-storey brick building on Mardol Head.

'S'-shaped braces in the framing, chevron and lozenge patterns, quatrefoils carved into the timbers, and distinctive twisted spiral shafts.

The influence of the Renaissance came late to Shropshire and only gradually made itself felt. Buildings became slightly more symmetrical and more attention began to be paid to scale and proportion. Three surviving buildings of the late sixteenth century are untypical for their date in their comparatively advanced design – and the fact that they were built of stone. Whitehall, a mansion off Abbey Foregate, was built of stones from the demolished abbey and is a very early example of a double-pile house. The Market Hall and former Grammar School boast naïve Renaissance decoration and are built of the pale grey Grinshill freestone that would be used so well two centuries later.

The belated arrival of brick to Shrewsbury was to change

20 Whitehall was built on land formerly owned by the abbey off what is now Monkmoor Road. It was built for a lawyer, Richard Prince, between 1578 and 1583, using stones from the demolished portions of the abbey complex. These were said to have been painted white, to hide their origins – hence the name. In architectural terms, it is claimed to be one of the very first 'double-pile' houses in England, and was certainly very sophisticated for Shrewsbury – and very rare in not being timber framed. It now houses the offices of the DSS. Its gatehouse, dovecot, and parts of the garden wall also survive.

21 The recumbent Dun Cow in Abbey Foregate has looked lazily down from her perch on the porch for many a year, but the building behind her is older still. Built as a house in the early seventeenth century, it only became a public house sometime in the eighteenth century. Now it is a pie shop that sells real ale.

22 The late-sixteenth-century Shrewsbury school of carpentry is seen at its best in the two portions of Owen's Mansion, built for a wool merchant in the 1590s. The typical motifs include quatrefoils sunk into the main timbers and created in the panel infills; cable-moulding – like giant upright barley sugar sticks – on the uprights; vine-leaf carving in the bargeboards; and decorative finials.

radically the look of the town. While chimneys were being built of brick by the middle of the sixteenth century, the earliest brick building in the vicinity is a wing of Albright Hussey on the northern outskirts, dated 1601. The first in Shrewsbury itself seems to have been Rowley's Mansion, built in 1618 but still to a very traditional design. Despite this, timber-framing continued well into the seventeenth century and, for poorer dwellings, for even longer, though few of these later examples have survived.

Shortly after 1660 some timber-framed buildings were given brick skins, such as the remarkable former Labour Club in Horsefair, Abbey Foregate, and the more elegant Kingston House in St Alkmund's Square. By the end of the century brick had become the only fashionable material to build with, and Shrewsbury has many fine examples of this date. If complete rebuilding in brick was too expensive, a brick façade was added.

23 Roger Rowley's son, William, built Rowley's Mansion next door to his father's old house in 1618. It was the first brick house to be built in the town, but was still fairly traditional in its multi-gabled design. For many years in the eighteenth century the vicar of St Chad's lived in the house, but it decayed rapidly in the early nineteenth century when it became used for commercial purposes. After many years of dereliction it was restored in 1983 and linked once again to Rowley's House as part of the borough museum.

24 The Porch House in Swan Hill was built ten years after the brick-built Rowley's Mansion, but was still timber framed. Dated 1628, it was built for Thomas Ridley and has a finely decorated doorway and a dated tie-beam. The porch which gave the house its name was removed for street widening many years ago. At one time it was used as a store for the adjacent police station but is now once again a house.

If even that was too costly, the old-fashioned timber frames were covered in lath and plaster and painted over. The new fashion called for flat symmetrical façades, sash windows, and, as the eighteenth century progressed, roofs hidden by parapets. The rich red bricks were all handmade locally, but with the arrival of the railways came mass-produced machine-made bricks from all over the country in different colours and surface finishes.

The end of the eighteenth century also saw the return of stone, even though it was only used as facing material – a very grand form of stone cladding. The easily worked and durable Grinshill stone, quarried a few miles to the north, was an ideal material for the rather severe neo-classical style of the later Georgian period. It was used in the rebuilding of St Alkmund's, new St Chad's, the Royal Infirmary and the Music Hall, among other prestigious projects. Those who could not afford stone cladding to their brick buildings could use stucco, a render finish lined to imitate ashlar. Shrewsbury has few examples, perhaps the best being a row of houses in Claremont Bank.

Not a great deal is known of the architects or craftsmen responsible for Shrewsbury's Georgian buildings. Thomas Farnolls Pritchard appears to have been the main influence in the mid-eighteenth century, designing the Foundling Hospital (now Shrewsbury School), rebuilding St Julian's, and building grand town houses such as Swan Hill Court and 6 Quarry Place. Several other buildings may be by Pritchard, including parts of the Lion Hotel, but proof is presently lacking. Later in the century John Gwynne designed the new English Bridge, George Steuart designed St Chad's, as well as Attingham Park a few miles to the west, and John Hyram Hancock was the first of three Hancocks working in the town.

The nineteenth century was a period of revivalism. Neo-Tudor, in brick or stone, was popular, along with neo-Gothic and even neo-Norman. Towards the end of the century the facing of new brick buildings with mock timber-framing became extremely popular in Shrewsbury. The buildings were nearly always too big, the details too crude, and the 'black-and-white' look bore no relation to the real thing, but they are still interesting in their own right. This fashion for the antique also resulted in lath and plaster being stripped off many real timber-framed buildings in the early twentieth century, and sympathetic restoration schemes,

25 Stuccoed terraces like this, in Claremont Bank, were very popular in jerry-built Regency buildings in seaside and inland resorts, from Margate to Cheltenham. This terrace, built in the early nineteenth century, is not, fortunately, jerry-built. Most stuccoed buildings were originally made to look like stone, and were only painted in white or pastel colours later on.

26 Thomas Farnolls Pritchard designed several town houses, though many of his buildings have yet to be positively identified. This one, in Quarry Place, is generally attributed to him and is typical of his style. Built in the 1760s, it shows how Georgian buildings had developed since the start of the century. In design, the top storey has been reduced to a half storey, above two full storeys, and the roof is now completely hidden behind a parapet. The windows are not as tall or narrow, are more deeply recessed, and the glazing bars are thinner.

27 Thomas Farnolls Pritchard designed the town house of the Marquis of Bath in the 1760s. It is a fairly conventional house when seen from Belmont, but its garden front has a hugh decorated pediment that would not be out of place in a country seat.

28 Parts of the Lion Hotel at the top of Wyle Cop are attributed to Pritchard, including the Adam-esque ballroom. The lion over the porch of this section dates from 1777 and is by John Nelson. The hotel was one of several important coaching inns in the town, and the arrival of a stage-coach up Wyle Cop must have been quite a sight.

29 Elegant Georgian houses line St John's Hill, ranging in date from the early to late eighteenth century. The streetscape is finished off beautifully by the clock tower of the 1960s Market Hall – that building's one saving grace.

such as the enlarging of the Plough in the Square. Competent local architects included S. Pountney Smith and A.E. Lloyd Oswell.

The last revival, at the turn of the century, was for the early Georgian or Queen Anne, a style favoured by the town's borough surveyor Arthur Ward. For over three decades until his retirement in 1945, Ward directly or indirectly protected the architectural heritage of the town. It was he that saved Rowley's House, now the museum, from demolition, and, when the English Bridge was replaced, he made sure that the old design was copied and the old facing stones were reused. When buildings were demolished for street widening, he designed neo-Georgian replacements. He was ahead of his time in many respects, realizing, for example, the importance of retaining original glazing bars and sparkling crown glass in Georgian

30 The 1960's telecom block may have looked acceptable on a greenfield site in Milton Keynes or in neighbouring Telford. However, it was built in the lowest part of a medieval town virtually next to the river, and completely spoils the view from Frankwell meadows and Coton Hill.

31 Rowley's House off Hill's Lane houses the borough museum but was only rescued from demolition in the 1920s by A.W. Ward. Roger Rowley, a London merchant, lived in the house at the end of the sixteenth century but the style suggests that it could date to the first half of the century. The building is unfortunately marooned in a sea of car parks.

32 The picturesque Plough Inn in the Square may look like a typical late sixteenth-century building but it is also an early example of conservation. The bottom two storeys of the building are certainly late sixteenth century but the second storey was only added at the turn of this century.

sashes. He also influenced the way in which other buildings were modernized, and although important buildings were inevitably lost, the damage done to Shrewsbury was far less than that in other historic towns.

Sadly the same cannot be said of the 1960s and 1970s. Few important buildings were lost in the large-scale developments of the period, but even the most mediocre of those that were demolished were better than their replacements. Many modern buildings are not bad in themselves, but simply lack any sympathy for the historic streetscapes of the town. New materials such as concrete, glass and plastic clash with the mellow brick and the timber frames. Bland horizontal horrors such as Woolworths and Littlewoods in Castle Street, and the new post office, were inserted into a traditional streetscape of tall, narrow buildings. Worse still was the redevelopment of the old Smithfield site

in Raven Meadows when the cattle market was moved to Harlescott in the 1960s. A wind-swept, concrete shopping centre was put up and, nearby, in the lowest part of the town, British Telecom built the town's only multi-storey building.

Since the end of the 1970s matters have generally improved, thanks to the activities of committed conservation officers, more sympathetic planners, public opinion, and an active Civic Society. The post-modernist buildings of today vary in quality and can only be fairly judged by posterity. Some seem to fit into the streetscape quite happily, but it has to be said that others, such as the new Charles Darwin Centre, seem, despite clear attempts at harmony, woefully out of place and simply too large for the town. At least, for the most part, the historic buildings are now treated with the respect and care that their antiquity deserves.

34 In an important regional town like Shrewsbury there has to be room for good quality new architecture, providing that it is in the right place. The Midland Printers' works in Harlescott achieves its quiet dignity through a careful choice of materials and attention to proportion.

Castle and Defences

One of the main ways the Normans maintained their stranglehold on the country was by the skilful use of the castle, a military innovation virtually unknown to the Saxons. At Shrewsbury the castle not only provided a centre from which to command the county and the borders, but also strengthened the only weak link in the town's defences. The dramatic setting of the castle was virtually destroyed when the railway station was built in the late 1840s.

No less than fifty-one houses had to be cleared away to make room for the castle, a fifth of the Saxon town. The first castle was probably a typical Norman motte-and-bailey, with a large mound, the motte, at one end of the compound and a defended enclosure, or bailey, below. On top of the motte would be a wooden tower or fighting platform, while in the bailey were all the domestic offices, barracks, stores and stabling.

Roger de Montgomery's younger son, Robert de Belesme, the third Earl of Shrewsbury, was banished for supporting a rebellion against Henry I, and Shropshire's virtual independence ended. The castle reverted to the Crown, and remained a royal possession for nearly five hundred years. In the civil war between Stephen and Matilda, Stephen's army took the castle after a month-long siege and put nearly a hundred of the defenders to the sword.

The earliest surviving portions of masonry are generally considered to date from the second half of the twelfth century, and include the main entrance to the castle with its plain round-headed arch and rounded jambs. As a strategic border castle in the wars against the Welsh, considerable amounts of money were spent on it. This did not prevent it falling to the Welsh in 1215, who then managed to hold the town for many months.

In the latter part of the thirteenth century the castle was rebuilt by Edward I, again as part of the English Crown's campaigns against the Welsh princes. Much of what remains is of this date, including the bulk of the hall and its two round towers. In 1283 the last Welsh prince, David ap Gruffydd, was captured and then brutally executed by Shrewsbury's High Cross. Edward's pacification of the Welsh ended in the following year with the signing of the Statute of Rhuddlan, and Shrewsbury's importance as a military base diminished. The castle fell into disrepair, and was ruinous by the end of the fourteenth century. In the 1530s Leland wrote, 'The castle hathe bene a strong thinge, it is now muche in ruine'.

After the town had been taken in 1215 it had become clear that the natural defences of the river Severn, even with the addition of the castle, were not good enough to protect it. There was probably already some form of defensive palisade but after

36 The Great Hall of Shrewsbury Castle, seen through the main entrance gate. After Robert de Belesme had been banished, the castle reverted to the Crown and was never the home of a powerful border baron again. It was ruinous by the end of the fourteenth century, repaired in the sixteenth and radically rebuilt two hundred years later by Thomas Telford, then on the threshold of his amazing career in civil engineering.

37 A good stretch of the town wall survives between Beeches Lane and St John's Hill, and the road behind the wall is called, logically, Town Walls. The thirteenth-century walls were radically repaired in 1951, but much of the original masonry survives.

Shrewsbury was recaptured Henry III ordered that the town be walled in stone. The townspeople were given a murage grant, that is, they were allowed to levy tolls on any goods being brought into the town to help pay for the new wall.

The whole circuit probably took over twenty years to complete, being finished around 1240. Although little of the wall is visible at first glance, much of it is substantially intact, hidden within later shops and houses. This is especially so in Castle Street and Pride Hill, where the wall ran along the ridge of high land overlooking what was then marshy ground by the river. The wall changed direction at Mardol and then ran up Claremont Bank and along another ridge in a broad sweeping curve towards the English Bridge. The best surviving stretch is to the west of the Quarry Park, which includes the only complete surviving mural tower – owned by the National Trust but not open to the public. The road

38 The only complete mural tower to survive in its entirety is in Town Walls. Once known as Wheeler's Tower, it now belongs to the National Trust but is not open to the public.

running along the inside of the wall is an unofficial inner bypass, and the low parapet appears to be quite insignificant. However, a glance over the side to the allotments below reveals the height of the much repaired and buttressed medieval town wall.

From the bottom of Wyle Cop the wall again ran along higher ground back towards the castle to complete the circuit. Several sections of the wall have been studied in depth; it was clearly an impressive fortification, well designed and well built up to 6 metres high in places. There were additional outworks in the defences, including parallel walls flanking a small lane leading down to the river near to the castle. The lane gets is name, St Mary's Water Gate, from a gate guarding the access to it from the river.

None of the impressive gates in the walls survive, nor the magnificent gatetowers that guarded the two medieval river bridges. A statue, said to be of the Duke of York, was salvaged from the old Welsh Bridge and placed at the north end of the Market Hall. At the opposite end is an angel taken from the castle gates.

Archaeological evidence indicates that the walls were soon allowed to fall into disrepair, and houses encroached upon them as early as the late fourteenth century. This reflected a peaceful era in Shrewsbury's history, interrupted only by the famous Battle of Shrewsbury of 1403 that took place just outside the town, and occasionally threatened by the prospect of Welsh uprisings.

Shrewsbury managed to escape any further military action until the English Civil War. Then the town was hurriedly refortified, with sections of the walls repaired, and new ditches and palisades added. The castle, the domestic parts of which appear to have been repaired some time in the late sixteenth century, was garrisoned for the King. For most of the war, Shrewsbury was an important Royalist base, but it fell eventually to the Commonwealth troops based at Wem in February 1645. These troops gained access with suspicious ease through St Mary's Water Gate, and quickly overcame the troops stationed in the town. The castle held out for a little while before surrendering, and a temporary fortification in Frankwell held out for a few hours more. Nevertheless, in less than a day one of Charles I's last major strongholds had fallen and the war was virtually lost.

After the Restoration the castle returned to private hands and was finally de-fortified in 1686 when the outer defences were pulled down. A century later the castle was again in a semi-ruinous state when it came into the hands of Sir William Pulteney who employed Thomas Telford to convert it into a house by subdividing the interior. Telford inserted the 'medieval' windows into the hall and built a folly, Laura's Tower, on top of the old motte. The castle remained private property until 1924 when the Shropshire Horticultural Society bought it and gave it to the borough. Most of Telford's internal alterations were removed and the Great Hall was restored. For many years the council met here, but now it contains a regimental museum. Despite its peaceful role it was badly damaged by terrorist bombs in 1992.

Most of the town gates were demolished towards the end of the eighteenth century as part of street improvement schemes, and several surviving sections of the walls and some mural towers went at the same time. For example, the building of new St Chad's in the 1790s led to the demolition of a long stretch of wall and one of the towers.

Churches

No visible traces remain of the five churches of pre-Conquest Shrewsbury, although the footings of a large apsed Saxon church were discovered beneath St Mary's in 1864. St Mary's, founded in the late tenth century, was the principal church by 1086, but it was not the earliest. That honour almost certainly belonged to old St Chad's, which was possibly dedicated to a former Bishop of Lichfield as early as the eighth century. St Alkmund's was probably founded two centuries later. The saint, a Northumbrian nobleman, was a particular favourite of Queen Aethelflaeda, and the church could well have been endowed by her in the new burh she was creating alongside the older settlement. All three of these churches were collegiate. This simply meant that canons or priests were attached to them who were to spread the word – in a similar way to the friar preachers who came several centuries later. The fourth church in the loop, St Juliana's, was not collegiate, fairly poorly endowed, and probably the last to be founded.

By the late Saxon period the churches in the loop were built of stone, unlike the fifth church over the English ford to the east, St Peter's. This was the gift of a rich Saxon, Siward, and was made of wood. However, its fortunes changed dramatically soon after the Conquest. The Normans were as ruthless in their piety as they were in war and transformed the religious life of the country both spiritually and architecturally. In Shrewsbury, Roger de Montgomery richly endowed a new Benedictine monastery on the site of St Peter's in the 1080s and, just a few days before his death, entered the abbey as a lay brother. The magnificent Norman church, dedicated to Saints Peter and Paul, was almost certainly built under the supervision of monks brought over from Normandy, and must have taken several decades to complete.

Although much altered over the years and radically reduced in size, parts of the interior can still evoke the impression of the

39 The doorway of St Mary's south porch dates to the late twelfth century, but the upper storey is later. The church recently became redundant and is being restored.

solid Norman work of the late eleventh century, with massive cylindrical piers and no-nonsense round arches in the nave and aisles. Of the other town centre churches, St Mary's has Norman work in the bottom of the tower, the transepts, and the south porch, but all this is later, probably from the late twelfth century. The base of St Julian's tower, and the partially exposed crypt of old St Chad's, are probably also pre-1200. Beyond the abbey to the east, a leper hospital was set up on the road to Wenlock in the mid-twelfth century and its chapel, St Giles, though heavily restored in the 1860s, still contains much Norman work.

In England, the Norman, or Romanesque, style gradually evolved into the first of the 'Gothic' styles – known as Early English – and the round arch gave way to the pointed. Between the two was a period of change whose architecture is called, logically enough, Transitional. The interior of St Mary's was remodelled in this style in the early thirteenth century, and the arcades between the nave and the new aisles are particularly fine. The clustered columns with their stiff-leaf capitals are virtually Early English, but the arches between are still round-headed.

Curiously, there are no obvious examples of true Early English work in the town, and only small pieces of the more florid style, the Decorated, that followed it from the end of the thirteenth century. The story is complicated because St Julian's was largely rebuilt in 1750, old St Chad's collapsed in 1788, and, in panic, most of St Alkmund's was pulled down soon afterwards. Thus three of the four principal medieval churches in the town were virtually destroyed in less than half a century. One church that does survive just to the north of the town, thanks to a restoration in the 1860s, is one dedicated to St Mary Magdalene. This was the church of the chantry college set up by Henry IV after the Battle of Shrewsbury in 1403 to pray for the souls of the slain; it was finished by 1409.

The grandest single architectural feature of any religious building in Shrewsbury has to be the magnificent west window of the abbey. Built in the late fourteenth century it is a fine early example of the last major phase of English Gothic – the Perpendicular. The abbey was radically rebuilt during this period and could well afford the expense. As a major landowner in the

40 A considerable amount of early Norman work survives inside Shrewsbury Abbey. The stilted type of round arch and the scalloped capitals are typical of the period around 1100.

area it profited from the agricultural prosperity of the times, and the abbot was a very important figure in local politics and also had a seat in the Lords.

As early as the start of the thirteenth century many clerics considered that the whole monastic system had lost its way and had ceased to cater for the real spiritual need of the people. This led to the creation of new orders of friars, sharing communal lives of absolute poverty dedicated to evangelism. The Dominicans, or Blackfriars, arrived in Shrewsbury in the early 1230s, the Franciscans, or Greyfriars, arrived in the mid-1240s, and the Austin Friars ten years later. All built their friaries within the loop but outside the walls. All that remains is a fragment of the Franciscan friary, near to Greyfriars Bridge, and the richly decorated windows clearly show that the friars too, by the early sixteenth century, had forgotten their professed humility.

40 Shrewsbury Abbey prospered until the late fourteenth century, which was probably when the magnificent west window was added. This is an early example of the Perpendicular style of English Gothic. After the dissolution in the 1530s, the nave and tower were saved from destruction because they were used as a parish church by the locals. The original Abbey Foregate goes to the left of the tower; Telford's early nineteenth-century bypass ploughed through monastic buildings to the right.

41 From this ornate early fourteenth-century pulpit a monk would read from the scriptures to his silent brethren eating in the refectory. It was cut off from the rest of the abbey by Telford's new road, and from the 1860s was in the Abbey Foregate railway station's yard. It was only given to the borough council for safekeeping in 1944.

The dissolution, a logical if brutal step in the English Reformation, followed shortly afterwards, and all the friaries, along with the abbey, were suppressed. The abbey may have been considered for cathedral status, but this did not come about, perhaps because the town was still suffering a long drawn out decline. However, because the nave of the abbey had served as the parish church for the people in the Abbey Foregate area, that at least was spared demolition. The rest of the magnificent church was pulled down and its stones quarried for new buildings, in particular for the nearby mansion of Whitehall. The claustral buildings to the south, including the infirmary, survived in part until Telford diverted the Abbey Foregate through them in the early nineteenth century. The infirmary survived even that, but was badly damaged in a fire of 1906 when it was part of a builder's store. Still standing, in romantic isolation, is the pulpit

42 St Alkmund's (left) and St Julian's have stood virtually side by side for over a thousand years. Both have some medieval work in their towers, but both were virtually rebuilt in the eighteenth century. St Julian's is now a thriving craft centre.

43 When it was decided to build a new St Chad's on a new site in the 1790s, George Steuart was chosen as the architect. Tradition has it that his controversial round-naved design was chosen by mistake from the final shortlist. It was consecrated in 1792.

43 The galleried round nave of George Steuart's neo-classical St Chad's is quite remarkable. This well-lit and airy church could accommodate two thousand people. The rather thin pillars are made of cast iron.

of the refectory. The church was restored and the east end rebuilt in the late 1880s by J.L. Pearson.

The religious and political uncertainty that followed the Reformation continued more or less until the end of the seventeenth century and, not surprisingly, very little new work was undertaken in remodelling the churches. The one charming exception to this is the small chapel in the grounds of Berwick House, just to the north-west of the town, built in 1672 alongside new alms-houses, which also remain.

In the early hours of 9 July 1788 the tower of old St Chad's collapsed. The church elders decided to build a new church on a new site, and only a fragment of the old building is left. The replacement church was built on the line of the town walls, overlooking the Quarry Park. It was designed by George Steuart and its most obvious feature is its round nave. Some say that Steuart

submitted several different designs and the round one was chosen by mistake. Claimed to be the largest round church in Britain, it was consecrated in 1792. The outside may be striking, but the inside, surprisingly spacious and well lit, is stunning. The fate of old St Chad's led indirectly to the demolition and rebuilding of most of St Alkmund's. Designed by Carline & Tilley and completed in 1795, the new nave and chancel are, externally, quite plain and dull. Its one interesting feature was its cast-iron window tracery. Although the fine painted east window has survived, most of the others were replaced a century later in stone.

The nineteenth century experienced what amounted to a religious revival, and in a growing town like Shrewsbury many new churches were needed to serve the needs of the new suburbs. The styles in the early part of the century varied from Carline's classical brick church of St Michael's in Spring Gardens to

44 John Carline's neo-classical St Michael's in Spring Gardens was built in brick and finished in 1830 at a cost of £2,000. In detail, if not in shape, it was clearly influenced by St Chad's. The chancel was added in 1873, and the church could then hold eight hundred people. It recently became redundant.

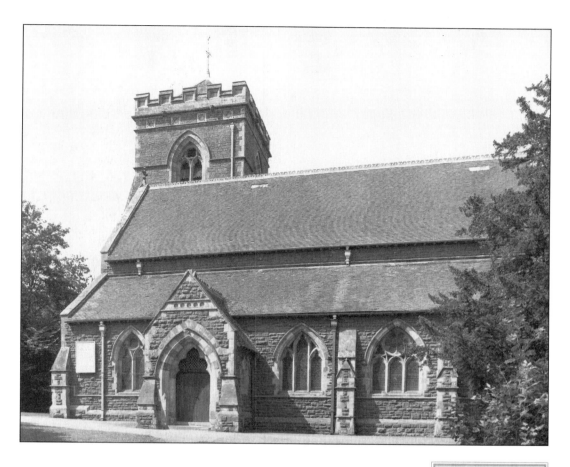

Haycock's rather dull stone neo-Gothic St George's in Frankwell. After changes in legislation in the mid-nineteenth century, Shrewsbury was chosen as the centre of a Roman Catholic bishopric. A cathedral, Our Lady of Mercy, was built on Town Walls by Edward Pugin, son of the more famous proponent of the Gothic revival, Augustus Welby Pugin. Lacking a tower because of problems with foundations, it was finished in 1856.

In the second half of the century neo-Gothic had become almost the universal style for all denominations, with the glorious exception of the Presbyterian church in Castle Gates designed by R.C. Bennett of Weymouth and built in 1870. Its somewhat tall and eccentric neo-Norman exterior was recently cleansed of a century's worth of grime, and the building has been converted into council offices. Architecturally it is truly ridiculous, but it has an ungainly charm all of its own. In contrast, the

45 From the outside, the younger Edward Haycock's Holy Trinity church, Meole Brace, is a good but conventional Gothic revival design, finished in 1868. Its glory lies in its windows, containing some of the best stained glass by William Morris and Edward Burne-Jones.

46 R.C. Bennett's Presbyterian church in Castle Gates was finished in 1870. Whatever its architectural merits it is certainly a building of character, and sand-blasting has enhanced its appearance. It was recently converted into offices.

47 The Wesleyan chapel in Swan Hill was rebuilt in a vaguely Italianate style in 1879 and is typical of its date. It is less typical of many other nonconformist chapels in still being used for its original purpose.

finest of the late Victorian churches was built just two years earlier in what was then the village of Meole Brace, now a suburb,
albeit a very independent suburb, of Shrewsbury. Holy Trinity
was designed by Edward Haycock junior in the grand Gothic
revival manner, but its main glories are the stained-glass windows by the famous William Morris & Company, considered to
be the best that they ever executed.

Shrewsbury also has many nonconformist chapels, virtually
all dating from the nineteenth and early twentieth centuries, and
many now used for other purposes. By that time the early sim-
plicity of such buildings had been lost and many were as ornate
as contemporary main-stream churches. Just over the English
Bridge, for example, the Congregational church in Abbey
Foregate of 1863 is a full-blown Gothic revival affair complete
with spire.

Public Buildings

Like most historic towns, Shrewsbury has always been proud of its public buildings. The oldest surviving buildings are also the best pair of their kind in the country – the new Market Hall in the Square, and the Grammar School (now the library) in Castle Gates. Both are well built in ashlared stone and their Renaissance details are sufficiently similar to suggest that they were both built by the same master mason. This is thought to have been Walter Hancock, who had designed the grand houses at High Ercall and Condover.

The Market Hall has an open ground floor with Tuscan columns, and remained in use as a market hall until 1869. On the ground floor a series of pegholes survives that used to mark the sale of the fleeces. When the old Welsh Bridge was demolished in the late eighteenth century, a statue of the Duke of York was salvaged from it and placed at one end of the building. The angel on the south side came from the old Castle Gate entrance to the town. The upper floor remains in civic use as the magistrates court but has become overcrowded, and new courts are being built on the outskirts of town.

The Grammar School was founded in 1552 but the present buildings were built, in two periods, in the 1590s and the 1630s. A medieval timber-framed building, Rigg's Hall, has a crownpost roof and was probably part of the first school. It was dismantled and rebuilt during the recent renovation work. The Grammar School had fluctuating fortunes but at times was one of the best schools in the kingdom. In the 1870s it was decided to move to a new site on Kingsland, built around the old

48 The Shoemakers' Arbour is dated 1679 and is really only the gateway to an 'arbour', or meeting place, for the shoemakers' guild on Kingsland. The statues are of Crispinian and Crispian, and the details are a fairly naïve attempt at the classical. The Shrewsbury Show gained a notoriety and was eventually stopped in the nineteenth century. The gateway was moved to the Dingle in 1879.

49 Known locally as the 'Dana', Shrewsbury Prison in Howard Street was designed by John Hiram Haycock and built by Thomas Telford between 1787 and 1793. Telford probably altered the design as he went along and is sometimes attributed with designing the gatehouse. The prison incorporated many of the ideas of Howard, the prison reformer, whose bust sits in the pediment and after whom the street was named.

50 The old Market Hall was built in Grinshill stone and opened in 1596. Its design is generally attributed to Walter Hancock, 'a mason of approved skyll and honestye'. In style it combines the traditional and rather naïvely executed Renaissance ideas but was worthy of its role as the commercial focus of the town. The building has continued to serve Shrewsbury to this day – for centuries as a market hall, and more recently as the magistrates court.

workhouse. The old school then became the town's library and museum. It was thoroughly renovated in the early 1980s and reopened as the main library in 1983.

The old workhouse on Kingsland had a very eventful life before it became part of what is now simply called Shrewsbury School. Designed by T.F. Pritchard it opened as an out-station of Captain Coram's London Foundling Hospital in 1760. It could take four hundred London orphans and train them for the textile trade, but closed in 1772. It was then used briefly as part of a woollen manufactory, and then held Dutch prisoners-of-war before it became the town's workhouse in 1784. In 1871 it closed and the school took it over. Sir Arthur Blomfield adapted the main building and added others, and the new school opened in 1882.

The town has several other interesting schools reflecting the architecture of their times. Bowdler's School in Beeches Lane is

51 Allatt's School was finished in 1800 at a cost of £2,000. It was designed by Haycock in a rather severe but elegant neo-classical manner and is faced with Grinshill stone. A bequest in the will of John Allatt, Gent., endowed a school for forty boys and forty girls. They were taught, separately, in the central block, and the headmaster and headmistress occupied the wings. It remained a school until the 1930s and was recently restored as offices.

52 Charles Darwin now sits outside the former Shrewsbury School built between the 1590s and 1630s.

53 Shrewsbury School moved to Kingsland in 1882. Blomfield remodelled the Foundling Hospital and added the chapel.

54 The former Priory School, in Priory Road, is now the Sixth Form College, a fine example of Queen Anne Revival of 1910.

55 Thomas Bowdler founded the school named after him in his will of 1724, built in Beeches Lane.

56 The Eye, Ear & Throat Hospital is a very loose interpretation of the neo-Gothic and the overall impression is somewhat overpowering. It is still used as a hospital, despite recent threats of 'rationalization'.

57 Hidden away at the end of a tree-lined avenue in Frankwell, Millington's Hospital is virtually unknown even to the locals. These almshouses were a bequest of Thomas Millington and originally built in 1748. They were subsequently rebuilt in 1794.

58 The Royal Salop Infirmary was one of the first large buildings in the country to have a hot water central heating system. It was closed in 1977 and has since been converted into a unique shopping centre, with luxury flats on the upper floors.

a typical early Georgian brick building, while Allatt's School on Murivance is a sterner stone-faced neo-classical structure of 1800. Both now have different uses. Near to Allatt's School is A.E. Lloyd Oswell's Girls High School, a mix of stone, brick and timber frame opened in 1897. By 1910 architectural fashion had come full circle, and the present Sixth Form College is a magnificent example of full-blown Queen Anne revival.

Shrewsbury had one of the first public infirmaries in the country, founded in 1747. In 1830 the new Royal Salop Infirmary in St Mary's Place opened, a severe stone building with a Doric portico designed by Edward Haycock the elder, and now a shopping centre and apartments. In complete contrast, the Eye, Ear & Throat Hospital on Town Walls, still in use, is a fiery red-brick and terracotta extravaganza of many styles. Clearly influenced by Waterhouse, but designed by C.O. Ellison of Liverpool, it opened in 1881.

59 The pretty cast-iron bandstand of 1879 in the Quarry Park is typical of many late-Victorian bandstands and was donated by the Shropshire Horticultural Society, who have been tremendous benefactors to the town over the years.

As well as public buildings to cater for trade, education and health, the town also had buildings for entertainment. In the eighteenth century it had bowling greens, a theatre and a race-course, none of which survive. The former theatre of 1833 off Bellstone is now a department store, but Haycock's neo-classical Music Hall of 1840 is still in use. A much earlier survival of public entertainment lies in the Quarry Park's Dingle. The late-seventeenth-century entrance to the Shoemaker's Arbour was moved from Kingsland, where it had been used in the boisterous shows that dated back to medieval times. The Victorian cast-iron bandstand nearby was donated by the Horticultural Society.

Modern public buildings no longer seem to aspire to grandeur. In 1964 the old Market Hall was replaced by a structure of brick, concrete and glass. Inside it is a lively place, full of bustle and bargains. Unfortunately from the outside it is, quite simply, ugly

60 The Music Hall in the Square was designed by Edward Haycock and has definite similarities with the Royal Salop Infirmary. The builder was Joseph Stant. Opened in 1840, it has an attached Ionic portico and is faced in Grinshill stone. It is still used for concerts and films, and now incorporates the medieval Vaughan's Mansion.

61 Lord Hill's Column (1814–16) is, at 41 metres, claimed to be the largest freestanding Greek Doric column in the world. It was built to commemorate one of Wellington's generals at Waterloo. Two architects and two builders were involved. Edward Haycock's original designs were altered by Thomas Harrison, and the original builder died in 1815 and was replaced by John Straphen, who donated the spiral staircase inside the column. The 5 metre statue of Lord Hill is by Joseph Panzetta and is made of Coade stone.

and totally unsympathetic in scale or materials to the older buildings around it. Only its square brick tower, a definite asset to the Shrewsbury skyline, saves it. On the edge of town, overlooked by Lord Hill's Column, the new Shire Hall struggles to aspire to anything – it is even difficult to know where the front door is.

Houses

One significant change seen in Shrewsbury and other similar towns in the twentieth century has been the gradual depopulation of the town centre as people move out to the suburbs and the outlying villages. Until the start of the century virtually every shop in the town had living quarters above it. Gradually most of these have been converted into offices or storerooms, but all too often others have been left disused. A traditional way of life dating back to the origins of the town is dying out at the very time when there is an acute shortage of affordable housing. The solution appears to be far too simple.

No Saxon houses survive, and only ephemeral traces have been found below ground. They would undoubtedly have been made of timber, and there were strict rules to prevent fire. If a house burnt down, the owner had to pay 40s. (£2) to the King and 2s. (10 pence) to each of his neighbours – a very large sum indeed. The Normans are known to have built stone houses elsewhere in the country, but no traces of any have ever been found in Shrewsbury. All the surviving Norman houses in Britain are built of stone, but these would have been in the minority. The basic plan was usually of a first-floor communal living space, the hall, over an undercroft, with other domestic ranges attached.

This type of arrangement still occurred until the fourteenth century, and Shrewsbury has substantial remains of two such houses, Benet's Hall and Vaughan's Mansion. Benet's Hall is sometimes called the Old Mint, being the traditional site of Charles I's Civil War mint. The 'tenement formerly called Bennetteshalle' is mentioned in a deed of 1378, and the building has been dated to the mid-thirteenth century. Vaughan's Mansion was badly damaged by fire early this century but was restored; it is now attached to the Music Hall. Other stone medieval houses are known to have existed, and the use of this expensive material

62 Hidden inside a clothes shop, the remains of Benet's Hall have a slightly different setting than most surviving thirteenth-century stone houses. It was clearly a very sophisticated house for its date, with rooms over an undercroft and a fireplace rather than an open hearth. This, for no real reason, was the supposed site of the Civil War mint, and it is still often called the 'Old Mint'.

63 The roof of the former first-floor hall of Vaughan's Mansion was rebuilt after a fire in 1917 to more or less the same design. It gives at least an idea of the grandeur of the medieval houses that Shrewsbury's rich wool merchants were building in the fourteenth century. It is now part of the Music Hall complex.

64 The garage in Abbey Foregate seems to be fairly ordinary until looked at more closely. It is, in fact, an almost complete medieval building in the shadow of the abbey itself, and in the foreground the base of one of its cruck frames can be seen.

for house building reflects the importance and prestige of the wool trade.

Other houses were composite structures, with a stone undercroft or semi-basement, and timber-framed upper floors. In several towns recent research has begun to unravel the riddle of high-status cellars surviving below much later buildings. It seems that these undercrofts were a combination of storeroom and showroom, built of stone to be fire and thief proof. One undercroft, in Pride Hill, was recently incorporated into a new McDonalds. Rigg's Hall was also restored recently and is part of the library complex. Unlike many medieval houses named after medieval owners, Rigg's Hall is named after a schoolteacher who lived there in the mid-nineteenth century.

From the fourteenth century onwards the first-floor hall went out of fashion, to be replaced by a large open ground-floor hall

65 The King's Head has a rather alarming, if eminently picturesque, lean because of an ill-thought change to the roof. Originally there were two roofs running at right angles to the street and ending in attic gables. At an unknown date these roofs were removed and a new roof, running parallel to the street, added. The building, restored in the 1920s and again in the 1980s, dates to the fifteenth century, and one traceried window may be real. Inside are some fine wall paintings.

66 This splendid screens passage bay behind the Nag's Head, Wyle Cop, is all that survives of a high-status late fourteenth-century house. It stood at the 'low' end of the open hall and is unusual in being, unlike the hall, of two storeys. The technical term for the nearest frame is a 'spere-truss'.

flanked by service and accommodation cross-wings at either end. In the typical layout, the main entrance was at the 'low' end of the hall next to the service wing. It led into a cross-passage, known as the screens passage, running across the bottom of the hall, and a fine example survives behind the Nag's Head in Wyle Cop. The rest of the late fourteenth- or early fifteenth-century building was only demolished a few years ago. This general medieval pattern had to be adapted in urban areas where space was at a premium and building plots tended to be narrow. Often the entire frontage at ground-floor level would be given over to shops, and the hall had to be tucked away to the rear, or, in several cases, placed on the first floor again. The Henry Tudor House on Wyle Cop, for example, had such a hall.

Another trend in the later medieval period was the speculative building of timber-framed terraces, with lodgings on the upper

68 A pomegranate provides unlikely evidence for the story that Mary Tudor stayed at the Olde House in Dogpole. It was amongst several other devices painted onto canvas and was part of the crest of Katherine of Aragon. Katherine, unfortunate first wife of Henry VIII, had lived at Ludlow briefly. The Olde House belonged to her servant, Anthony Rocke. Most of the house probably dates to the early sixteenth century, but the fine doorway is later.

floors and shops below, the two not necessarily rented by the same tenants. The grandest and most obvious example of this type of arrangement is the Abbot's House in Butcher Row, of about 1500. Said to have belonged to the Abbot of Lilleshall and used as his town house, its monastic links are tenuous despite the grandeur of its carving. It retains many of its original ground-floor shop fronts, the oldest in the town.

By the late sixteenth century domestic life had become less communal and more private, so that the layout of houses had changed considerably since medieval times. Life had previously revolved around the hall, often the only heated room in the house and the place where meals were eaten and where servants slept. By the end of Elizabeth's reign most houses of any size had separate rooms for eating and sleeping in, as well as private rooms for 'withdrawing' to – drawing-rooms and parlours. The old

(text continues on p. 84)

69 The Abbot's House in Butcher Row is wrongly named and was certainly not the town house of the Abbot of Lilleshall, despite local tradition. This speculative row of dwellings above individual shops could, however, have been built by the abbey sometime before the dissolution to raise revenue. The shop fronts to the right are medieval but much of the framing above has been patched and altered over the years.

70 This close-studded gable in Mardol is rather unusual for Shrewsbury. It lacks any decoration whatsoever but is very substantially built. It probably dates to the early sixteenth century, but it seems rather too severe in style to have been a house.

71 This building on the corner of Mardol and Hill's Lane appears to have been built in the late sixteenth century, but then had two full-height square bay windows added to it in the seventeenth century. These were only restored to their original glory at the end of the 1980s by a local firm of conservation architects. Note how the side frame is quite plain, and how all the decoration was 'up front'.

72 During the Civil War Prince Rupert spent some time in Shrewsbury and lived in this house on Church Street, Jones' Mansion. It had been built in the early seventeenth century by Thomas Jones, six-times bailiff. Originally it had an open courtyard onto St Mary's Street, but this was built over in the eighteenth century. Its timber framing had been covered up for many years before the plaster was removed in 1908.

73 By no means the largest, but probably the finest, of all the timber-framed buildings in Shrewsbury is the Jacobean Council House Gateway, dated 1620. It still has some typical Shrewsbury School motifs but also has more up-to-date Renaissance features, such as the carved pilasters flanking the gateway itself. The Council House beyond was an outstation of the Council of the Marches. Actually based in Ludlow, this effectively controlled much of the border region until the Civil War.

74 This is one of the most intriguing buildings in Shrewsbury but little is known about its history. It faced the old market place, the Horsefair, in Abbey Foregate and is mainly timber framed. However, it was then faced on two sides by this remarkable brickwork and given a new, overhanging, roof. Dating it is difficult, but it was probably built in the mid-seventeenth century, perhaps not long after the Restoration. It is the earliest surviving example in the town of a brick façade that makes a real attempt at classicism.

medieval garderobe chutes in the largest houses had in general given way to privy chambers. All these features can be seen in Shrewsbury's fine collection of timber-framed buildings of the period, though later changes have often considerably altered their interiors to cater for changing circumstances.

In the centuries that followed, most changes were to do with architectural fashions and materials. The medieval tradition of having living quarters above ground-floor shops continued, and completely normal houses were built in the middle of town whose only difference from purely domestic buildings elsewhere was their commercial ground floors. It is also important to remember that by no means all houses in the middle of town had shops at all, many only being adapted for such purposes in the later nineteenth century.

The demand for town houses by the gentry in the eighteenth century led to more speculative building. The cheapest form of

(text continues on p. 90)

75 Another early piece of brickwork is Kingston House in St Alkmund's Square, also fronting a timber-framed building. It dates to the later part of the seventeenth century and has a fine, if technically incorrect, door-case. The window above the door is blind. In the background is one of the few late eighteenth-century windows of St Alkmund's that has kept its cast-iron tracery.

76 When the Earl of Bradford built himself a town house in Dogpole in 1696 he had first to remove a timber-framed house on the site. The new house was in fashionable brick and virtually square in plan. It was called Newport House, after the Earl's family name. The porch is a later edition, probably early nineteenth century, and is actually made of iron. The house is now called the Guildhall and is the main office of the borough council.

77 The house removed from the Newport House site was re-erected a few hundred yards away near to the entrance to the castle – moving timber-framed buildings is clearly not a twentieth-century phenomenon. Castle Gates House is said to have been the home of Lord Bradford's mistress. The framing was covered with plaster and the bays were probably added to it during rebuilding. The plaster was removed when the house was restored in 1912.

78 The vogue for brick meant that timber frames were definitely considered to be old fashioned. If a brick façade was too expensive, the frames were simply plastered over, and one or two, such as the Cromwell Hotel in Dogpole, still are. The building is probably of early seventeenth-century date, but the sashes may have been added when the front was covered.

79 In one instance, brick was even added to clad a partially stone-built building. This odd range on the corner of Dogpole and Church Street is very difficult to date and could be late seventeenth or early eighteenth century. Part of it is now the Loggerheads public house, but its original function is uncertain.

80 Tucked away off School Gardens, this brick house was probably built at the end of the seventeenth century. Its steep overhanging roof, its graceful Flemish gable, and its windows, taller than those of the true Georgian period, all point to such an early date. Later houses have been butted against it and some of its upper windows have been blocked.

81 One of the most ambitious examples of brick fronting in the region has to be the south front added to various buildings of the Council House courtyard. Three storeys high with an additional row of blank attic 'windows', it has some Flemish influence and must date to the start of the eighteenth century.

building was the terrace, a style already used previously but one that had become very popular because of its use in fashionable spa towns like Bath and Cheltenham. Shrewsbury also had a spa, at Sutton, but it did not really take off. Notable surviving terraces in the fashionable area near the Quarry Park include the Crescent and Claremont Buildings of the mid-1790s, an early nineteenth-century row in Claremont Bank, and Crescent Place, opposite the Crescent and probably of the 1840s. Further afield more humble terraces were being built for the middle classes and, much humbler still, for the workers.

The terrace and the peculiarly English 'semi' were the most significant features of the rapid growth of the town in the later part of the nineteenth century. Most of the new brick houses were built, often badly, by property speculators but some were built by freehold land societies. The mass production of architectural ornaments –

82 The Lion & Pheasant at the bottom of Wyle Cop is a good quality hotel, probably much older than its rendered early eighteenth-century façade would suggest. The 'Good Stabling' is now for cars.

(text continues on p. 97)

83 This brick front was added to a timber-framed building in Abbey Foregate, north of the abbey, very early on in the eighteenth century. The quality of the carved brick aprons to the windows is extremely good, and this feature is not seen anywhere else in the town. Sadly, time has taken its toll on the building and alterations to it have not been kind.

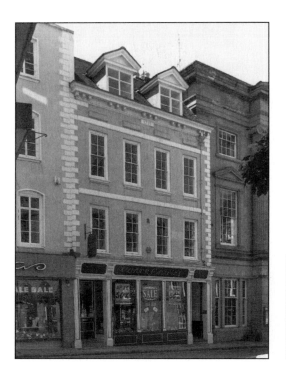

84 This building of 1713 looks fairly simple but its design is quite sophisticated and subtle. Note, for example, how the modillions, or brackets, under the eaves of the roof run in groups of three between the window bays below, and how the projecting panels above the second floor windows harmonize with the recessed panels below them.

85 This three-storey building in Princess Street, just off the Square, is rather unusual. The raised parapet hides a very steep-pitched roof, possibly suggesting that the building behind the façade is somewhat older. The window surrounds are almost Baroque in their details and are not seen on any other Shrewsbury building. The front dates from the early eighteenth-century, and inside the tea-shop on the first floor full-height panelling of that date survives.

86 One of the best examples of brick-cladding to a timber frame in the county. In the late sixteenth century a good quality timber-framed house was built alongside Milk Street, just east of old St Chad's church. In the mid-eighteenth century, this was fronted by a taller, symmetrical brick façade with a central pediment in a very watered down Palladian style. At the end of the building, the raised upper-storey walls were built directly on top of the old gable rafters. By the end of the century this part of Milk Street had been renamed Belmont.

87 Hardwick House on St John's Hill is perhaps the most ambitious of the Georgian town houses built in the first half of the eighteenth century. The quality of the workmanship is superb and the house, dated to around 1730, is really a country house in miniature. It even has flanking stables and carriage sheds on either side, with Flemish gables. These are, appropriately, now used to stable cars.

88 Shrewsbury's answer to the great crescents of eighteenth-century Bath is not quite on the same scale. The brick-built Crescent, in Town Walls, consists of just four houses in a very plain, curving terrace finished in about 1795. The main decorative features are the Adam-inspired fanlights above the doors, matched by blind fanlights above the ground-floor windows. In the foreground is a surviving section of town wall.

89 Carline & Tilley built Claremont Buildings near to the new St Chad's church in the mid-1790s as a speculative venture; it has an austere neo-classical style and is faced with Grinshill stone. The first houses in the short terrace were ready by 1794. In front of the houses is a railed 'area', a London feature allowing light to enter the basement windows.

90 The Mount, off the Mount in Frankwell, is a typical plain yet elegant late-Georgian house, standing alone in its grounds. It was built in the late 1790s on the then edge of the town by a Dr Darwin, and his son the famous naturalist Charles Darwin was born here in 1809.

91 A typical street of late nineteenth-century artisans' houses in Greenfields, a new estate of the 1880s and 90s laid out in a grid pattern just north of the town centre. Greenfields had its own school, its own chapel, and its own shop. Well-tended gardens are very much a feature of Shrewsbury.

from keystones to moulded bricks – added some variation to what were fairly standard designs. The nearest Shrewsbury came to having its own 'garden suburb', a feature of many towns in the early twentieth century, was the Sentinel Village in Harlescott laid out by Alley & MacLellan when they set up their factory in the First World War. The relatively large houses, in short terraces, were well built and full of all mod-cons, including hot water, and set a fine standard. The first council houses, built from 1910 in Wingfield Gardens, were equally well thought out and spacious. Inter-war housing in areas like Monkmoor was clearly influenced by A.W. Ward's love of the Georgian. Later council housing after the Second World War perhaps became too concentrated on large estates, lacking variety and charm. The same, in fairness, can also be said of much of the new private housing estates that have sprung up rapidly since the 1960s, but at least Shrewsbury has been spared the high-rise.

92 The datestone gives the relevant details for this house in School Gardens – SB 1825. SB was Dr Samuel Butler, long-serving and influential headmaster of the nearby school. The Tudor-revival style, although in brick, matched the original school itself.

93 Oakley Manor, to the south of the town centre on Belle Vue Road, was built by the local architect Samuel Pountney Smith who specialized in churches and alms-houses. Built around the 1850s its design recreated medieval windows and Tudor framing. It also includes salvaged timbers from real timber-framed buildings, including an early seventeenth-century staircase and a datestone of 1596. The house is now used as borough council offices.

94 In the late nineteenth century all sorts of styles and revivals were tried, but local architect A.E. Lloyd Oswell's offices for the Halifax Building Society in the High Street stand out from the crowd. Its lavishly decorated 'Northern Renaissance' style would be more at home on the canal banks of Antwerp or Amsterdam than in the Welsh marches.

95 The former Co-op building in Castle Street is a very late example of the 'timber-framed revival'. Totally over the top – too large, too many styles, too many different materials and too coarse detailing – it is at least interesting in a way that so many modern buildings are not. It is not really a building that warrants preservation.

96 The controversial Lloyds Bank at the bottom of Pride Hill replaced a mock-timber-frame in the 1960s. It is brutally modern, yet still respects the basic scale of the town and reflects aspects of its timber-framed neighbours. Love it or loathe it, the building makes a positive contribution to the streetscape.

Industrial
Buildings

Shrewbury's wealth has always been, and still is, mainly based on marketing rather than manufacturing, and it has few surviving industrial buildings of note. However, those that it does have are of sufficient importance to warrant preservation, and include one of the most important industrial buildings in the world.

There are very few reminders of just how important a transport highway the river Severn once was, apart from the 'dry' arches of the two main bridges that took the tow-paths. Plans to link the Severn with other rivers were never finished. When the Shrewsbury Canal opened in 1796 it only linked up with the canals of East Shropshire, which could only take small 'tub' boats. It was not until 1834 that narrowboats from the national network could reach Shrewsbury, and in the following year a new Butter Market was built at the Howard Street terminus. Designed by Fallows & Hart of Birmingham, this very functional building was given a fine neo-classical façade. It later became a railway goods shed and was slightly altered in 1900 when the station was enlarged. After several years of dereliction it was converted into a popular night-club in 1987.

In 1848 the belated arrival of the railways in Shrewsbury effectively killed off the river trade and took away much of the canal's traffic. The four companies constructing lines to the town agreed to build a joint station. It was designed in a vague but effective neo-Tudor style by a local architect, Thomas Penson, and built in Grinshill stone. All additions made to it since have been in the same style, and when the station was enlarged at the end of the nineteenth century, a new floor was

97 The Butter Market was built in 1835 at the Howard Street terminus of the Shrewsbury Canal, and later became a railway warehouse. Saved from demolition in 1974 and restored ten years later, it is now a night-club. The odd alignment of the nearest wall was due to alterations to the road at the turn of the century which were connected with the enlarging of the nearby station.

98 Shrewsbury's magnificent neo-Tudor railway station was finished in 1849 and then enlarged several times. The last major extension was at the turn of the century, when a complete new floor was added *under* the original ground floor. It was designed by Thomas Penson, who designed all the stations on the line to Chester. After many years of dereliction it was restored in the mid-1980s.

added below the original ground floor. British Rail allowed the building to become derelict and in 1967 planned to demolish it. Fortunately it was saved, and in 1986 BR moved their regional offices back from the ugly 1960s block on Chester Street to the lovingly restored station, now recognized as an architectural gem of the railway system. Just to the east of the station is the largest manual signal box still in use in Britain, but it is in the middle of the busy Severn Bridge Junction and there is no public access to it.

By far the most important industrial building in Shrewsbury is in the north of the town, in Ditherington, and was built as a flax mill in 1797 by the side of the new canal. In the eighteenth century the area around modern-day Ironbridge was probably the most technologically advanced area in the world, particularly with anything to do with iron. Iron was first successfully smelted with coke, rather than with charcoal; the area produced the first iron railway wheels, the first iron rails, the first successful iron boat, and, of course, the first iron bridge of any size. However, in Ditherington Mill, Shrewsbury can boast an iron 'first' that is just as important – no less than the world's first iron-framed building, the forerunner of the skyscrapers that now dominate the skylines of the world's great cities.

Fire was an ever present threat in any textile mill, and towards the end of the eighteenth century different ideas were being tried to make mills more fire-resistant. The main problem was the amount of timber used, particularly in the floors. When Charles Bage designed Ditherington Mill for the firm of John Marshall's & Sons, he introduced cast-iron beams, supported by cast-iron pillars. The beams supported brick arches that in turn supported solid floors without any timber in them; the roof was also supported on similar arches, with slates directly laid on top of them. Although the outside walls of the mill were still entirely of brick, the principle for iron framing had been set. The mill continued to work flax until 1886 and then became a maltings, which resulted in changes in the window patterns. It finally closed a century later and for several years this Grade I listed building has lain derelict. A sensible plan to relocate the scattered borough council offices in the mill was recently turned down by the councillors. Bage designed a similar flax mill in Castlefields shortly afterwards,

99 The former Shropshire Maltings in Ditherington closed in 1987 and this, one of the most important industrial buildings in the world, now lies derelict.

100 The new Welsh Bridge replaced a medieval structure further upstream. It was designed by Carline & Tilley and finished in 1795. Telford had warned that the new site would be subject to scouring by the river and was proved right. Additional measures had to be taken in 1833 to improve the footings. In the balustrade above the central arch is a pulley, once used to help pull trows upstream.

101 Porthill Bridge crosses the river by the Quarry Park and looks to be a typical late-Victorian suspension bridge. It was actually built, in steel, in 1922.

but this was pulled down in the 1830s. However, its iron-framed store in Severn Street survives, imaginatively converted into a terrace of three-storey houses in the 1850s.

Coleham was quite an industrial suburb. For centuries there were corn mills on the Rea Brook, originally built by the abbey, and it had short-lived woollen and cotton industries. The links for Telford's Menai suspension bridge of 1826 were forged in Hazeldine's foundry, parts of which remain. The large locomotive depots of the GWR and LNWR, and the Abbey Works where electric trams were once made, have all been flattened fairly recently. The pumping station, built at the turn of the century, still has its pair of Renshaw-built steam engines that worked up until the 1970s, and is the subject of a long-term preservation scheme. Most of the industrial development is now to the north of the town, in Harlescott, started by Alley &

103 Alley & MacLellan came to Shrewsbury in the First World War and built a factory and model village in which to house their workers. After the Second World War the factory was owned by Rolls-Royce and by Perkins, but now belongs to Vickers. It is a shame that their new sign couldn't fit in with the symmetry of the gatehouse.

MacLellan of Glasgow. They built what became the Sentinel Waggon Works, home of the famous Sentinel steam waggons and locomotives. Few of the new industrial buildings have any great architectural value, though there are one or two notable exceptions.

Further Reading

Local Books

Carr, A.M. *Shrewsbury As It Was* (1978)
Cromarty, D., *Everyday Life in Medieval Shrewsbury* (1990)
Garner, L., *The Buildings of Shropshire: Vol II, The Tudor and Stuart Legacy 1530–1730* (1989)
Garner, L., *The Buildings of Shropshire: Vol III, The Georgian and Regency Legacy 1730–1840* (1990)
Hobbs, J.L., *Shrewsbury Street-Names* (reprint 1982)
de Saulles, M., *The Book of Shrewsbury* (1986)
Stratton, M., *Shrewsbury Town Trail* (1989)
Trinder, B. (ed.), *Victorian Shrewsbury* (1984)

General Books

Brunskill, R.W., *Timber Building in Britain* (1985)
Brunskill, R.W., *Brick Building in Britain* (1990)
Clifton-Taylor, A., *The Pattern of English Building* (4th edn 1987)
Cossons, N., *The BP Book of Industrial Archaeology* (1987)
Cruickshank, D., *A Guide to the Georgian Buildings of Britain & Ireland* (1985)
Harris, R., *Discovering Timber-Framed Buildings* (1978)
Pevsner, N., *The Buildings of England* series, in county volumes (various dates)
Platt, C., *The English Medieval Town* (1976)